IT'S TIME TO EAT CHEESY FIESTA POTATOES

It's Time to Eat CHEESY FIESTA POTATOES

Walter the Educator

SKB

Silent King Books

A WhichHead Entertainment Imprint

Disclaimer

This book is a literary work; the story is not about specific persons, locations, situations, and/or circumstances unless mentioned in a historical context. Any resemblance to real persons, locations, situations, and/or circumstances is coincidental. This book is for entertainment and informational purposes only. The author and publisher offer this information without warranties expressed or implied. No matter the grounds, neither the author nor the publisher will be accountable for any losses, injuries, or other damages caused by the reader's use of this book. The use of this book acknowledges an understanding and acceptance of this disclaimer.

Little potato cubes, cozy and hot,

A yummy treat we just can't stop.

Golden and soft, with cheese on top,

Cheesy fiesta potatoes, a tasty delight!

It's time for a snack that's warm and bright,

It's Time to Eat

Cheesy Fiesta Potatoes

CHEESY FIESTA POTATOES

It's Time to Eat CHEESY FIESTA POTATOES is a collectible early learning book by Walter the Educator suitable for all ages belonging to Walter the Educator's Time to Eat Book Series. Collect more books at WaltertheEducator.com

USE THE EXTRA SPACE TO TAKE NOTES AND DOCUMENT YOUR MEMORIES

Radiance of True Pursuit

Chasing stars in twilight's glow,
With every step, our spirits soar.
A journey full of highs and lows,
With every loss, we yearn for more.

In passion's fire, we find our way,
Through shadows deep and valleys wide.
With courage bright, we choose to stay,
In the heart of dreams, we bide.

The road may twist, the path may weave,
Yet purpose leads us, strong and true.
In every breath, we dare believe,
That light will pierce the heavy blue.

Through struggle's lens, we see the grace,
Of every moment, hard-fought gain.
In true pursuit, we find our place,
United in our joy and pain.

Dreams Woven in Diligence

In quiet moments, visions glow,
Where hope and labor intertwine.
Each step a stitch, in softest flow,
A tapestry of dreams divine.

With steady hands, we shape the light,
Through trials faced, our spirits rise.
Patience sown, we claim our fight,
In fields of effort, wisdom lies.

Each dawn we wake, with purpose clear,
Chasing shadows, casting doubt.
With every heartbeat, let us steer,
Towards horizons, wide and stout.

For dreams are born from seeds we sow,
In gardens rich, of time and care.
Through diligence, together grow,
A harvest bright, beyond compare.

ABOUT THE CREATOR

Walter the Educator is one of the pseudonyms for Walter Anderson. Formally educated in Chemistry, Business, and Education, he is an educator, an author, a diverse entrepreneur, and he is the son of a disabled war veteran. "Walter the Educator" shares his time between educating and creating. He holds interests and owns several creative projects that entertain, enlighten, enhance, and educate, hoping to inspire and motivate you. Follow, find new works, and stay up to date with Walter the Educator™

at WaltertheEducator.com

Cheesy fiesta potatoes make us smile!

A snack so tasty, soft and mild

It's Time to Eat

Cheesy Fiesta Potatoes

Each little cube goes down so fast.

From the first bite to the very last,

Cheesy fiesta potatoes are such a treat!

Soft and golden, warm and neat,

These cheesy potatoes beyond compare!

So let's all cheer, it's time to share,

They make every meal feel just right.

A warm and cheesy, savory bite,

Cheesy fiesta potatoes are joy unbound.

It's Time to Eat

Cheesy
Fiesta
Potatoes

With friends or family gathered around,

We eat them up without a care!

A spoonful here, a spoonful there,

Cheesy potatoes can't be beat.

For lunch, a snack, or dinner treat,

With every spoonful, it feels so great!

It's like a party on our plate,

Each little bite makes us smile wide.

Sometimes with a dab of sour cream,

Every bite fills us with delight.

It's Time to Eat

Cheesy Fiesta Potatoes

The golden cheese, the fluffy inside,

Cheesy potatoes are the best to eat!

A fiesta of flavors, warm and sweet,

They taste like a cheesy, savory dream.

With cheese so gooey, soft and bright,

Eating these potatoes is so much fun!

We scoop them up, one by one,

A plate of joy in every form.

Cheesy and creamy, smooth and warm,

Adds a bit of flavor we love so much.

A sprinkle of spices, just a touch,

A fiesta of taste to hold and hold!

With each little bite, flavors so bold,

Covered in cheese, melted a lot.